THE RIME OF THE ANCIENT MARINER

THE RIME OF THE ANCIENT MARINER

by
Samuel Taylor Coleridge

Illustrations by Gustave Doré

SCHOOL OF TOMORROW®

Lewisville, Texas

ISBN 1-56265-016-5

2 3 4 5   Printing/Year   97 96 95 94

Printed in the United States of America

INTRODUCTION

The Rime and Its Times

Born in England in 1772, Samuel Taylor Coleridge grew up in an age of discovery. As the world's leading maritime power, Britain was in the forefront of an international race to discover, claim, and chart any and all new lands and seas around the globe.  In oaken sailing ships equipped with the latest navigational instruments, intrepid skippers, inquisitive scientists, and hardy sailors left Britain's shores on journeys that sometimes lasted several years.

Thus, the appearance of *The Rime of the Ancient Mariner* in 1797 was well timed. Although the ballad was dismissed at first by literary critics, it gained instant, widespread popularity with the British public. An entertaining ballad with a sobering message for an age groping for spiritual realities, *The Rime* is still, after nearly two hundred years, one of the best-known and best-loved poems in the English language.

About the Illustrator

Born in the French province of Alsace, Gustave Doré (1832-1883) moved to Paris at the age of fifteen. Although Doré set his hand to painting and sculpting, it was in engraved illustrating that he was most successful. His illustrations—finely executed and vast in quantity— reflect an enjoyment of a wide variety of subjects. Towards the end of his life, Mr. Doré became interested in religion. His illustrations for *The Rime of the Ancient Mariner* were produced in this period, as were his fascinating scenes from the Bible and *Paradise Lost* by poet John Milton.

North
America

South
America

Afr

Equator

The Marine

out
hom
cou

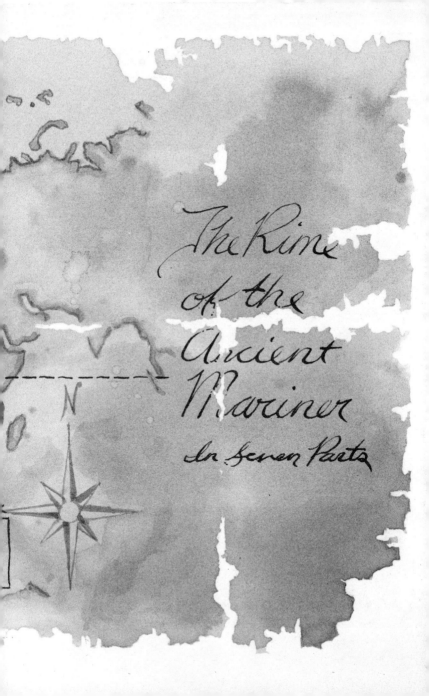

The Rime
of the
Ancient
Mariner
In Seven Parts

PART ONE

It is an ancient Mariner,
And he stoppeth one of three.
"By thy long gray beard and glittering eye,
Now wherefore stopp'st thou me?

"The Bridegroom's doors are opened wide, 5
And I am next of kin;
The guests are met, the feast is set;
May'st hear the merry din."

He holds him with his skinny hand,
"There was a ship," quoth he. 10
"Hold off! unhand me, gray-beard loon!"
Eftsoons his hand dropt he.

12 eftsoons: at length.

The Wedding Guest is spellbound by the eye of the old seafaring man and constrained to hear his tale.

He holds him with his glittering eye—
The Wedding Guest stood still,
And listens like a three years' child;   15
The Mariner hath his will.

The Wedding Guest sat on a stone;
He cannot choose but hear;
And thus spake on that ancient man,
The bright-eyed Mariner.   20

"The ship was cheered, the harbour cleared,
Merrily did we drop
Below the kirk, below the hill,
Below the lighthouse top.

The Mariner tells how the ship sailed southward with a good wind and fair weather till it reached the Line.*

"The Sun came up upon the left,   25
Out of the sea came he!
And he shone bright, and on the right
Went down into the sea.

"Higher and higher every day,
Till over the mast at noon—"   30
The Wedding Guest here beat his breast,
For he heard the loud bassoon.

23 kirk: church.
* equator

4

*The Wedding
Guest heareth
the bridal
music; but the
Mariner
continueth his
tale.*

The bride hath paced into the hall,
Red as a rose is she;
Nodding their heads before her goes   35
The merry minstrelsy.

The Wedding Guest he beat his breast,
Yet he cannot choose but hear;
And thus spake on the ancient man,
The bright-eyed Mariner.   40

---

36 minstrelsy: musicians.

*The ship driven
by a storm
toward the
South Pole.*

"And now the Storm blast came, and he
Was tyrannous and strong;
He struck with his o'ertaking wings,
And chased us south along.

"With sloping masts and dipping prow,   45
As who pursued with yell and blow
Still treads the shadow of his foe,
And forward bends his head,
The ship drove fast, loud roared the blast,
And southward aye we fled.   50

"And now there came both mist and snow,
And it grew wondrous cold;
And ice, mast-high, came floating by,
As green as emerald.

"And through the drifts the snowy clifts   55
Did send a dismal sheen;
Nor shapes of men nor beasts we ken—
The ice was all between.

"The ice was here, the ice was there,
The ice was all around;   60
It cracked and growled, and roared and howled,
Like noises in a swound!

---

55 drifts: mists. **55 clifts:** icebergs.
57 ken: have knowledge of. **62 swound:** a faint.

"At length did cross an Albatross,
Thorough the fog it came;
As if it had been a Christian soul,   65
We hailed it in God's name.

"It ate the food it ne'er had eat,
And round and round it flew.
The ice did split with a thunder fit;
The helmsman steered us through!   70

"And a good south wind sprung up behind;
The Albatross did follow,
And every day, for food or play,
Came to the mariners' hollo!

"In mist or cloud, on mast or shroud,   75
It perched for vespers nine;
Whiles all the night, through fog-smoke white,
Glimmered the white moonshine."

64 thorough: through. **67 eat:** pronounced *et*, the old form of *eaten*. **75 shroud:** rope of the rigging. **76 vespers:** evenings.

The ancient
Mariner
inhospitably
killeth the pious
bird of good
omen.

"God save thee, ancient Mariner!
From the fiends, that plague thee thus!—   80
Why look'st thou so?"—With my crossbow
I shot the Albatross.

79-81 "God ... so?": the Wedding Guest says this.

PART TWO

"The Sun now rose upon the right;
Out of the sea came he,
Still hid in the mist, and on the left   85
Went down into the sea.

"And the good south wind still blew behind,
But no sweet bird did follow,
Nor any day for food or play
Came to the mariners' hollo!   90

His shipmates cry out against the ancient Mariner for killing the bird of good omen.

"And I had done a hellish thing,
And it would work 'em woe;
For all averred, I had killed the bird
That made the breeze to blow.
'Ah wretch!' said they, 'the bird to slay,   95
That made the breeze to blow!'

18

*They justify the
same, and make
themselves
accomplices in
the crime.
The fair breeze
continues; the
ship enters the
Pacific Ocean,
and sails
northward.*

"Nor dim nor red, like God's own head,
The glorious Sun uprist;
Then all averred, I had killed the bird
That brought the fog and mist.   100
'Twas right,' said they, 'such birds to slay,
That bring the fog and mist.'

"The fair breeze blew, the white foam flew,
The furrow followed free;
We were the first that ever burst   105
Into that silent sea.

*The ship hath
been suddenly
becalmed.*

"Down dropt the breeze, the sails dropt down,
'Twas sad as sad could be;
And we did speak only to break
The silence of the sea!   110

"All in a hot and copper sky,
The bloody Sun, at noon,
Right up above the mast did stand,
No bigger than the Moon.

"Day after day, day after day,   115
We stuck, nor breath nor motion;
As idle as a painted ship
Upon a painted ocean.

*And the
Albatross
begins to be
avenged.*

"Water, water, everywhere,
And all the boards did shrink;   120
Water, water, everywhere,
Nor any drop to drink.

98 uprist: arose. **104 furrow:** wake of a ship. **114 Moon:** the
sun when seen through a haze seems very small.

"The very deep did rot:—
That ever this should be!
Yea, slimy things did crawl with legs   125
Upon the slimy sea.

"About, about, in reel and rout
The death fires danced at night;
The water, like a witch's oils,
Burnt green and blue and white.   130

"And some in dreams assurèd were
Of the spirit that plagued us so;
Nine fathom deep he had followed us
From the land of mist and snow.

"And every tongue, through utter drought,   135
Was withered at the root;
We could not speak, no more than if
We had been choked with soot.

"Ah! welladay! what evil looks
Had I from old and young!   140
Instead of the cross, the Albatross
About my neck was hung.

127 rout: tumultuous crowd. **128 death fires:** St. Elmo's fires,
a luminous charge of electricity sometimes appearing on a
ship's rigging or masts. Superstitious sailors believed it to be
an omen of disaster. **134 land of mist and snow:** regions
around Cape Horn, South America. **139 welladay:** alas.

PART THREE

The ancient Mariner beholdeth a sign in the element afar off.

"There passed a weary time. Each throat
Was parched, and glazed each eye.
A weary time! a weary time!   145
How glazed each weary eye,
When looking westward, I beheld
A something in the sky.

"At first it seemed a little speck,
And then it seemed a mist;   150
It moved and moved, and took at last
A certain shape, I wist.

"A speck, a mist, a shape, I wist!
And still it neared and neared;

At its nearer approach it seemeth him to be a ship, and at a dear ransom he freeth his speech from the bonds of thirst.

As if it dodged a water sprite,   155
It plunged and tacked and veered.

"With throats unslaked, with black lips baked,
We could nor laugh nor wail;
Through utter drought all dumb we stood!
I bit my arm, I sucked the blood,   160
And cried, 'A sail! a sail!'

"With throats unslaked, with black lips baked,
Agape they heard me call;

A flash of joy.

Gramercy! they for joy did grin,
And all at once their breath drew in,   165
As they were drinking all.

And horror follows. For can it be a ship that comes onward without wind or tide?

"'See! see!' (I cried) 'she tacks no more!
Hither to work us weal;
Without a breeze, without a tide,
She steadies with upright keel!'   170

164 Gramercy: great thanks. **168 work us weal**: help us.

24

"The western wave was all aflame.
The day was well-nigh done!
Almost upon the western wave
Rested the broad bright Sun;
When that strange shape drove suddenly   175
Betwixt us and the Sun.

"And straight the Sun was flecked with bars,
(Heaven's Glory send us grace!)
As if through a dungeon grate he peered
With broad and burning face.   180

"'Alas!' (thought I, and my heart beat loud)
'How fast she nears and nears!

Are those her sails that glance in the Sun,
Like restless gossameres?

"'Are those her ribs through which the Sun   185
Did peer, as through a grate?
And is that Woman all her crew?
Is that a Death? and are there two?
Is Death that woman's mate?'

"Her lips were red, her looks were free,   190
Her locks were yellow as gold:
Her skin was as white as leprosy,
The Nightmare Life-in-Death was she,
Who thicks man's blood with cold.

"The naked hulk alongside came,   195
And the twain were casting dice;
'The game is done! I've won! I've won!'
Quoth she, and whistles thrice.

184 gossameres: floating webs. **190 free:** wild.

26

No twilight within the courts of the Sun.

"The Sun's rim dips; the stars rush out;
At one stride comes the dark;   200
With far-heard whisper, o'er the sea,
Off shot the specter bark.

At the rising of the Moon.

"We listened and looked sideways up!
Fear at my heart, as at a cup,
My lifeblood seemed to sip!   205
The stars were dim, and thick the night,
The steersman's face by his lamp gleamed white;
From the sails the dew did drip—
Till clomb above the eastern bar
The horned Moon, with one bright star   210
Within the nether tip.

One after another.

"One after one, by the star-dogged Moon,
Too quick for groan or sigh,
Each turned his face with a ghastly pang,
And cursed me with his eye.   215

His shipmates drop down dead.

"Four times fifty living men,
(And I heard nor sigh nor groan)
With heavy thump, a lifeless lump,
They dropped down one by one.

But Life-in-Death begins her work on the ancient Mariner.

"The souls did from their bodies fly—   220
They fled to bliss or woe!
And every soul, it passed me by,
Like the whiz of my crossbow!"

---

202 specter: ghostly.
209 clomb: climbed. **210 horned:** crescent.

28

PART FOUR

The Wedding Guest feareth that a spirit is talking to him.

"I fear thee, ancient Mariner!
I fear thy skinny hand!   225
And thou art long, and lank, and brown,
As is the ribbed sea sand.

But the ancient Mariner assureth him of his bodily life, and proceedeth to relate his horrible penance.

"I fear thee and thy glittering eye,
And thy skinny hand, so brown."—
"Fear not, fear not, thou Wedding Guest!   230
This body dropt not down.

"Alone, alone, all, all alone,
Alone on a wide wide sea!
And never a saint took pity on
My soul in agony.   235

He despiseth the creatures of the calm.

"The many men, so beautiful!
And they all dead did lie:
And a thousand thousand slimy things
Lived on; and so did I.

And envieth that they should live, and so many lie dead.

"I looked upon the rotting sea,   240
And drew my eyes away;
I looked upon the rotting deck,
And there the dead men lay.

"I looked to Heaven, and tried to pray;
But or ever a prayer had gusht,   245
A wicked whisper came, and made
My heart as dry as dust.

245 or: before.

"I closed my lids, and kept them closed,
And the balls like pulses beat;
For the sky and the sea, and the sea and the sky   250
Lay like a load on my weary eye,
And the dead were at my feet.

But the curse
liveth for him in
the eye of the
dead men.

"The cold sweat melted from their limbs,
Nor rot nor reek did they;
The look with which they looked on me   255
Had never passed away.

"An orphan's curse would drag to hell
A spirit from on high;
But oh! more horrible than that
Is the curse in a dead man's eye!   260
Seven days, seven nights, I saw that curse,
And yet I could not die.

"The moving Moon went up the sky,
And nowhere did abide;
Softly she was going up,   265
And a star or two beside—

"Her beams bemocked the sultry main,
Like April hoarfrost spread;
But where the ship's huge shadow lay,
The charmèd water burnt alway   270
A still and awful red.

267 **main**: sea.

34

*By the light of
the Moon, he
beholdeth
God's creatures
of the great
calm.*

"Beyond the shadow of the ship,
I watched the water snakes:
They moved in tracks of shining white,
And when they reared, the elfish light   275
Fell off in hoary flakes.

"Within the shadow of the ship
I watched their rich attire:
Blue, glossy green, and velvet black,
They coiled and swam; and every track   280
Was a flash of golden fire.

*Their beauty
and their
happiness. He
blesseth them in
his heart.*

"O happy living things! no tongue
Their beauty might declare.
A spring of love gushed from my heart,
And I blessed them unaware.   285
Sure my kind saint took pity on me,
And I blessed them unaware.

*The spell begins
to break.*

"The selfsame moment I could pray;
And from my neck so free
The Albatross fell off, and sank   290
Like lead into the sea.

36

PART FIVE

"Oh sleep! it is a gentle thing,
Beloved from pole to pole!
To Heaven's King the praise be given!
He sent the gentle sleep from Heaven,   295
That slid into my soul.

The ancient Mariner is refreshed with rain.

"The silly buckets on the deck,
That had so long remained,
I dreamt that they were filled with dew;
And when I awoke, it rained.   300

"My lips were wet, my throat was cold,
My garments all were dank;
Sure I had drunken in my dreams,
And still my body drank.

"I moved, and could not feel my limbs;   305
I was so light—almost
I thought that I had died in sleep,
And was a blessèd ghost.

He heareth sounds and seeth strange sights and commotions in the sky and the elements.

"And soon I heard a roaring wind;
It did not come anear,   310
But with its sound it shook the sails,
That were so thin and sere.

"The upper air burst into life!
And a hundred fire flags sheen,
To and fro they were hurried about!   315
And to and fro, and in and out,
The wan stars danced between.

---

297 silly: useless. **312 sere:** dried up. **314 fire flags sheen:** lightning flashes. **313-317 "The upper ... between.":** The Mariner sees the aurora australis, or southern lights.

"And the coming wind did roar more loud,
And the sails did sigh like sedge:
And the rain poured down from one black cloud;   320
The Moon was at its edge.

"The thick black cloud was cleft, and still
The Moon was at its side;
Like waters shot from some high crag,
The lightning fell with never a jag,   325
A river steep and wide.

*The bodies of
the ship's crew
are inspired,
and the ship
moves on.*

"The loud wind never reached the ship,
Yet now the ship moved on!
Beneath the lightning and the Moon
The dead men gave a groan.   330

"They groaned, they stirred, they all uprose,
Nor spake, nor moved their eyes;
It had been strange, even in a dream,
To have seen those dead men rise.

"The helmsman steered, the ship moved on;   335
Yet never a breeze upblew;
The mariners all 'gan work the ropes,
Where they were wont to do;
They raised their limbs like lifeless tools—
We were a ghastly crew.   340

"The body of my brother's son
Stood by me, knee to knee;
The body and I pulled at one rope,
But he said nought to me."

319 sedge: tall, coarse grass. **322 cleft:** split. **338 wont:**
accustomed.

"I fear thee, ancient Mariner!"   345
"Be calm, thou Wedding Guest!
'Twas not those souls that fled in pain,
Which to their corses came again,
But a troop of spirits blest;

"For when it dawned—they dropped their arms,   350
And clustered round the mast;
Sweet sounds rose slowly through their mouths,
And from their bodies passed.

"Around, around, flew each sweet sound,
Then darted to the Sun;   355
Slowly the sounds came back again,
Now mixed, now one by one.

"Sometimes adropping from the sky
I heard the skylark sing;
Sometimes all little birds that are,   360
How they seemed to fill the sea and air
With their sweet jargoning!

"And now 'twas like all instruments,
Now like a lonely flute;
And now it is an angel's song,   365
That makes the heavens be mute.

"It ceased; yet still the sails made on
A pleasant noise till noon,
A noise like of a hidden brook
In the leafy month of June,   370
That to the sleeping woods all night
Singeth a quiet tune.

348 corses: corpses. **362 jargoning:** confused singing.

42

"Till noon we quietly sailed on,
Yet never a breeze did breathe;
Slowly and smoothly went the ship,   375
Moved onward from beneath.

"Under the keel nine-fathom deep,
From the land of mist and snow,
The Spirit slid; and it was he
That made the ship to go.   380
The sails at noon left off their tune,
And the ship stood still also.

"The Sun, right up above the mast,
Had fixed her to the ocean.
But in a minute she 'gan stir,   385
With a short uneasy motion—
Backwards and forwards half her length
With a short uneasy motion.

"Then like a pawing horse let go,
She made a sudden bound;   390
It flung the blood into my head,
And I fell down in a swound.

*The Polar
Spirit's fellow
demons, the
invisible
inhabitants of
the element,
take part in his
wrong: and two
of them relate,
one to the
other, that
penance long
and heavy for
the ancient
Mariner hath
been accorded
to the Polar
Spirit, who
returneth
southward.*

"How long in that same fit I lay,
I have not to declare;
But ere my living life returned,   395
I heard and in my soul discerned
Two voices in the air.

"'Is it he?' quoth one, 'Is this the man?
By Him who died on cross,
With his cruel bow he laid full low   400
The harmless Albatross.

"'The Spirit who bideth by himself
In the land of mist and snow,
He loved the bird that loved the man
Who shot him with his bow.'   405

"The other was a softer voice,
As soft as honeydew;
Quoth he, 'The man hath penance done,
And penance more will do.'"

PART SIX

First Voice
"'But tell me, tell me! speak again,   410
Thy soft response renewing—
What makes that ship drive on so fast?
What is the ocean doing?'

Second Voice
"'Still as a slave before his lord,
The ocean hath no blast;   415
His great bright eye most silently
Up to the Moon is cast—

46

"'If he may know which way to go;
For she guides him smooth or grim.
See, brother, see! how graciously   420
She looketh down on him.'

First Voice

*The Mariner
hath been cast
into a trance,
for the angelic
power causeth
the vessel to
drive
northward
faster than
human life
could endure.*

"'But why drives on that ship so fast,
Without or wave or wind?'

Second Voice

"'The air is cut away before,
And closes from behind.   425

"'Fly, brother, fly! more high, more high!
Or we shall be belated:
For slow and slow that ship will go,
When the Mariner's trance is abated.'

*The
supernatural
motion is
retarded: the
Mariner
awakes, and his
penance begins
anew.*

"I woke, and we were sailing on   430
As in a gentle weather;
'Twas night, calm night, the moon was high;
The dead men stood together.

"All stood together on the deck,
For a charnel dungeon fitter;   435
All fixed on me their stony eyes,
That in the Moon did glitter.

"The pang, the curse, with which they died,
Had never passed away;
I could not draw my eyes from theirs   440
Nor turn them up to pray.

435 charnel dungeon: burial vault.

"And now his spell was snapt; once more
I viewed the ocean green,
And looked far forth, yet little saw
Of what had else been seen—   445

"Like one, that on a lonesome road
Doth walk in fear and dread,
And having once turned round, walks on,
And turns no more his head;
Because he knows, a frightful fiend   450
Doth close behind him tread.

"But soon there breathed a wind on me,
Nor sound nor motion made;
Its path was not upon the sea,
In ripple or in shade.   455

"It raised my hair, it fanned my cheek
Like a meadow gale of spring—
It mingled strangely with my fears,
Yet it felt like a welcoming.

"Swiftly, swiftly flew the ship,   460
Yet she sailed softly too:
Sweetly, sweetly blew the breeze—
On me alone it blew.

"Oh! dream of joy! is this indeed
The lighthouse top I see?   465
Is this the hill? is this the kirk?
Is this mine own countree?

"We drifted o'er the harbour bar,
And I with sobs did pray—
'O let me be awake, my God!   470
Or let me sleep alway.'

"The harbour bay was clear as glass,
So smoothly it was strewn!
And on the bay the moonlight lay,
And the shadow of the Moon.   475

"The rock shone bright, the kirk no less,
That stands above the rock;
The moonlight steeped in silentness
The steady weathercock.

The angelic
spirits leave the
dead bodies

"And the bay was white with silent light,   480
Till rising from the same,
Full many shapes, that shadows were,
In crimson colours came.

And appear in
their own forms
of light.

"A little distance from the prow
Those crimson shadows were.   485
I turned my eyes upon the deck—
Oh,—what I saw there!

473 **strewn:** spread

52

"Each corse lay flat, lifeless and flat,
And, by the holy rood!
A man all light, a seraph man,   490
On every corse there stood.

"This seraph band, each waved his hand;
It was a heavenly sight!
They stood as signals to the land,
Each one a lovely light.   495

"This seraph band, each waved his hand,
No voice did they impart—
No voice; but oh! the silence sank
Like music on my heart.

"But soon I heard the dash of oars,   500
I heard the Pilot's cheer;
My head was turned perforce away
And I saw a boat appear.

"The Pilot and the Pilot's boy,
I heard them coming fast.   505
Dear Lord in Heaven! it was a joy
The dead men could not blast.

"I saw a third—I heard his voice;
It is the Hermit good!
He singeth loud his godly hymns   510
That he makes in the wood.
He'll shrive my soul, he'll wash away
The Albatross's blood."

---

489 rood: cross (the cross of Christ). **490 seraph:** angel.
502 perforce: by necessity. **512 shrive** (shrīv): absolve from
sin.

PART SEVEN

The Hermit of the wood

"This Hermit good lives in that wood
Which slopes down to the sea.   515
How loudly his sweet voice he rears!
He loves to talk with mariners
That come from a far countree.

"He kneels at morn, and noon, and eve—
He hath a cushion plump: 520
It is the moss that wholly hides
The rotted old oak stump.

"The skiff boat neared; I heard them talk,
'Why, this is strange, I trow!
Where are those lights so many and fair,   525
That signal made but now?'

Approacheth the ship with wonder.

"'Strange, by my faith!' the Hermit said—
'And they answered not our cheer!
The planks look warped! and see those sails,
How thin they are and sere!   530
I never saw aught like to them,
Unless perchance it were

"'Brown skeletons of leaves that lag
My forest brook along;
When the ivy tod is heavy with snow,   535
And the owlet whoops to the wolf below,
That eats the she-wolf's young.'

"'Dear Lord! it hath a fiendish look—'
(The Pilot made reply)
'I am afeared'—'Push on, push on!'   540
Said the Hermit cheerily.

524 trow (trō): believe; think. **528 cheer:** call; hail.
535 ivy tod: ivy bush.

"The boat came closer to the ship,
But I nor spake nor stirred;
The boat came close beneath the ship,
And straight a sound was heard.   545

"Under the water it rumbled on,
Still louder and more dread;
It reached the ship, it split the bay,
The ship went down like lead.

"Stunned by that loud and dreadful sound,   550
Which sky and ocean smote,
Like one that hath been seven days drowned
My body lay afloat;
But swift as dreams myself I found
Within the Pilot's boat.   555

"Upon the whirl, where sank the ship,
The boat spun round and round;
And all was still, save that the hill
Was telling of the sound.

"I moved my lips—the Pilot shrieked   560
And fell down in a fit;
The holy Hermit raised his eyes,
And prayed where he did sit.

"I took the oars; the Pilot's boy,
Who now doth crazy go,   565
Laughed loud and long, and all the while
His eyes went to and fro.
'Ha! ha!' quoth he, 'full plain I see,
The Devil knows how to row.'

545 straight: immediately.

58

"And now, all in my own countree,   570
I stood on the firm land!
The Hermit stepped forth from the boat,
And scarcely he could stand.

The ancient
Mariner
earnestly
entreateth the
Hermit to
shrive him, and
the penance of
life falls on
him.

"'O shrive me, shrive me, holy man!'
The Hermit crossed his brow.   575
'Say quick,' quoth he, 'I bid thee say—
What manner of man art thou?'

"Forthwith this frame of mine was wrenched
With a woeful agony,
Which forced me to begin my tale;   580
And then it left me free.

60

And ever and anon throughout his future life an agony constraineth him to travel from land to land.

"Since then, at an uncertain hour,
That agony returns;
And till my ghastly tale is told,
This heart within me burns.   585

"I pass, like night, from land to land;
I have strange power of speech:
That moment that his face I see,
I know the man that must hear me;
To him my tale I teach.   590

"What loud uproar bursts from that door!
The wedding guests are there.
But in the garden-bower the bride
And bridemaids singing are;
And hark the little vesper bell, 595
Which biddeth me to prayer!

"O Wedding Guest! this soul hath been
Alone on a wide wide sea;
So lonely 'twas, that God himself
Scarce seemed there to be.   600

"O sweeter than the marriage feast,
'Tis sweeter far to me,
To walk together to the kirk
With a goodly company!—

"To walk together to the kirk,   605
And all together pray,
While each to his great Father bends,
Old men, and babes, and loving friends,
And youths and maidens gay!

And to teach by
his own
example love
and reverence
to all things that
God made and
loveth.

"Farewell, farewell! but this I tell   610
To thee, thou Wedding Guest!
He prayeth well who loveth well
Both man and bird and beast.

"He prayeth best who loveth best
All things both great and small;   615
For the dear God who loveth us,
He made and loveth all."

The Mariner, whose eye is bright,
Whose beard with age is hoar,
Is gone; and now the Wedding Guest   620
Turned from the bridegroom's door.

He went like one that hath been stunned,
And is of sense forlorn.
A sadder and a wiser man,
He rose the morrow morn.   625

S. T. Coleridge